THE
WORRY-FREE
PARENT

WORKBOOK

T0335197

Also by Sissy Goff

Raising Worry-Free Girls
Braver, Stronger, Smarter
Brave

Coauthored with Melissa Trevathan and David Thomas

Raising Boys and Girls
Are My Kids on Track?
Intentional Parenting

Coauthored with Melissa Trevathan

Modern Parents, Vintage Values
Raising Girls
The Back Door to Your Teen's Heart

THE WORRY-FREE PARENT

WORKBOOK

LIVING IN CONFIDENCE SO YOUR KIDS CAN TOO

Sissy Goff, *LPC-MHSP*

BETHANYHOUSE

a division of Baker Publishing Group
Minneapolis, Minnesota

Published by Bethany House Publishers
Minneapolis, Minnesota
www.bethanyhouse.com

Bethany House Publishers is a division of
Baker Publishing Group, Grand Rapids, Michigan

Printed in the United States of America

ISBN 978-0-7642-4103-1 (trade paper)
ISBN 978-0-7642-4208-3 (casebound)
ISBN 978-1-4934-4221-8 (ebook)

Unless otherwise indicated, Scripture quotations are from THE HOLY BIBLE, NEW INTERNA-TIONAL VERSION®, NIV® Copyright © 1973, 1978, 1984, 2011 by Biblica, Inc.® Used by permission. All rights reserved worldwide.

Scripture quotations marked ESV are from The Holy Bible, English Standard Version® (ESV®), copyright © 2001 by Crossway, a publishing ministry of Good News Publishers. Used by permission. All rights reserved. ESV Text Edition: 2016

Scripture quotations marked THE MESSAGE are taken from THE MESSAGE, copyright © 1993, 2002, 2018 by Eugene H. Peterson. Used by permission of NavPress. All rights reserved. Represented by Tyndale House Publishers, Inc.

Scripture quotations marked NASB are taken from the (NASB®) New American Standard Bible®, Copyright © 1960, 1971, 1977, 1995, 2020 by The Lockman Foundation. Used by permission. All rights reserved. www.lockman.org

Some names and recognizable details have been changed to protect the privacy of those who have shared their stories for this book.

Illustrations on pages 29 and 106 by Connie Gabbert.

Cover design by Dan Pitts

The author is represented by Alive Literary Agency, www.aliveliterary.com

23   24   25   26   27   28   29   7   6   5   4   3   2   1

Contents

Why This Book?   7

Introduction   11

SECTION 1 **Understanding the Past**

1. Understanding Worry and Anxiety   21

2. Understanding Ourselves   35

3. How Anxiety Impacts You   50

4. How Your Anxiety Impacts Your Kids   60

SECTION 2 **Help for the Present**

5. Help for Your Body   75

6. Help for Your Mind   85

7. Help for Your Heart   99

8. Help for Your Kids   111

SECTION 3 **Hope for the Future**

9. Admit Failure. Know Grace.   123

10. Try Softer   132

11. Trust Your Gut   138

12. Trust God   144

Notes   155

Why This Book?

Hi! I'm so grateful and honored you chose to buy this workbook. My hope in writing *The Worry-Free Parent* was to come as close as possible to making it feel like you were sitting in my office as you were reading the book. But we know that a book is more monologue than dialogue. And my hope was to create conversation. This workbook gives us much more space to do that—to not only create conversation, but to dig deeper and more thoughtfully into what being a worry-free parent really means. Some text will be familiar, but much of the content goes beyond what's included in *The Worry-Free Parent* with the hope that you feel free to do the same.

I have a counselor I see for myself, when I need it, who happens to be pretty tough. Exceedingly kind, but tough. When I refer others to her, I always say that I didn't quite understand I was a sinner until I started going to her for counseling. I did from a theological perspective, but not nearly as much from a personal one. Every time I went in with hurt feelings at the hand of a friend, she would make me look at my part in it. I am so grateful. I also remember seeing one of my favorite musicians in her lobby once, and thinking, *Wow. I liked her before, but I really like her now that I know she can hang in there with this therapist.* Now, don't get me wrong. Right alongside a hard look into my sin and struggles, I saw so much grace. More grace than I ever could have imagined. I understood Jesus' love for me better every single time I left her office. My hope is that this workbook helps you in much the same way.

I want us to take a hard, deep look together. And I want you to find so much grace in the process. Grace and freedom are the goal here. And for you to feel like who you are as a parent is more than enough. Because it is. God chose you for each of your kids. He knew what he was doing. I want you to know, as you read this book, that you do too. I'm proud of you for picking it up and can't wait to see what God does in and through you as you make your way through the prompts and pages.

Here are a few directions as we start this journey together:

1. Be kind to yourself.

The purpose of this workbook is to uncover more of what keeps us stuck in worry. It is going to be hard sometimes. It will likely bring up things you might not love about who you are as a person or as a parent. Be kind to yourself in those moments. That's not where we're going to stay. There is so much good news coming and so much good about who you are. We're all just a messy mixture of both. One of my all-time favorite quotes is from a poet named Kahlil Gibran, who says, "The deeper that sorrow carves into your being, the more joy you can contain."[1] We're headed for a lot of joy together.

2. Go slow.

I hope that this workbook can be a transformative tool in your life to help you become the parent you not only long to be, but God made you to be. Transformation does not happen quickly. No new parent by Friday here. Let yourself read slowly and pray and think through the answers to the prompts. Take your time. Let your heart catch up with what God is uncovering in you. There is so much good that is going to emerge.

3. Be kind to yourself.

Yes, still.

4. Be kind to your parents.

I met with a fellow counselor a few months ago who sees a lot of clients in their early twenties. "They're at that juncture," she said, "when they're discovering more of who they are and all the things their parents did wrong." I laughed when she said it because I not only remember going through that myself, but I have watched thousands of young adults do the same. As you look back at your childhood and learn more of what you might have missed, your first tendency may be to blame your parents. For all of us, it's important to process the feelings we might not have been allowed to feel or that we didn't have room to process as we were growing up. For some of you, those feelings may need to be talked through with your parents. There is past hurt that needs to be addressed still. Some of you may not be able to process that hurt with your parents because of too-early loss or even toxic relationships that wouldn't be safe to address. But for many of us, I believe our parents were doing the very best they could with what they had. They didn't have a lot back then. There was not a lot of support for parents or education on how to be a better parent. So if that's the case for your family of origin, I want you to look at your parents with eyes of grace as well—just like I want you to look at yourself.

5. If it stirs up more, I'd like for you to see a counselor.

If issues arise that feel bigger than the pages of a workbook can address, I'd like for you to call a therapist. If feelings come up that you're just not sure what to do with, it would be a good idea to call a therapist. If you want to process more with a person who can give you tips specifically geared toward you and your kids, a therapist would be a great person to have on your team. I wish every person had what one parent called a "back pocket counselor"—a person you could see to talk things through with as they come up along the way. They will come up for every single one of us. I remember a mom telling me that counseling had been scaffolding for her and her family. You need scaffolding. And, again, you need a whole lot of kindness and grace.

6. Be kind to yourself.

Yes, it's that important.

I am so grateful and impressed that you're embarking on this journey. Thank you for the privilege of allowing me to come alongside you. Your work in these pages—your thoughtfulness, your time, and the heart that you pour in—will be a gift not just to you, but a profound gift to your children. I know it. I think you will soon too.

Introduction

I met with a mom this week who said these words to me: "I just don't trust myself as a parent. If I was doing it right, my child wouldn't act like this." Let's dispel that myth right here . . . or, actually, all the myths contained within that statement.

1. There is no right way to do it.
2. Your child's behavior is not a direct reflection of your effectiveness as a parent.
3. If I could give you anything as you work your way through this workbook, it would be the confidence to trust yourself as a parent. And to trust that God is in it with you.

We're going to talk through all those ideas as we journey together throughout this workbook. But *if you were to say right now what your worries are, what would they be?*

Do you trust yourself as a parent?

Why or why not?

The opening story in *The Worry-Free Parent* book is about the parent who told me she needed to hear that what she was feeling was normal and that she's doing a great job. *What do you need to hear today?*

I want you to practice saying those things out loud to yourself. Yes, I am serious. Say them out loud right now . . . either where you are sitting or in front of a mirror. If I were sitting with you, I'd say them directly to you. Also, just in case they're not on the list you just wrote, what you're feeling is normal AND you're doing a great job. Yes, you.

We all need to be reminded of truth . . . especially those of us who are worriers. *Besides the truth you just reminded yourself of, what is one truth you could hang on to today?* It could be a Scripture or one of your favorite quotes. Or even just a statement. Write that truth here. You could even tear it out and hang it on your mirror or use it as a bookmark in the book you're currently reading. I want you to be reminded of it often.

I'm going to include a worry-fighting Scripture at the end of each chapter to give you truth to ponder. I believe truth is *that* important in our fight against worry. We're also going to include a section in each chapter called Gratefuls, Hopefuls, and Truthfuls—because having gratitude, having hope, and remembering truth can all make a profound difference for us in this journey. In those sections, I want you to include three things you're grateful for, three things that currently bring you hope, and three truths you want to remember, whether those truths are Scripture, quotes you love, or things you're learning. Gratitude, hope, and truth are three of the most important tools to have as we fight the anxiety that is all too pervasive in our world and homes.

I'll repeat what I wrote in the introduction of *The Worry-Free Parent:*[1]

Because I meet with kids, I also spend a lot of time with parents. In the past few years, there has been one issue I've talked about the most with both: anxiety. You may have read the statistics already. At the time I'm sitting down to write this book, one in four kids is dealing with anxiety. Because I've been seeing more and more kids facing this issue, I've tried to do a deep dive to help. At this time, I've read thirty-five books on the subject, become certified as an anxiety specialist twice over, and written three books about it already. Those books are about your kids. One is for the elementary-aged girls in your life, called *Braver, Stronger, Smarter*. One is for the middle and high school girls, titled *Brave*. And one is for you and about all those girls, *Raising Worry-Free Girls*. This book, however, is the first book specifically *about you*. Of all of the things I've learned about anxiety, potentially the most important is this: Anxiety is an isolator, but it's certainly not an isolated issue. It has an amazing ability to spread. In almost every situation in which I've had an anxious child or teen in my office, they have had at least one anxious parent. Now, that's from my observation. The research says that if you have anxiety as a parent, your child is seven times more likely to deal with it themself.[2]

Has anxiety been an isolator in your life? ☐ *Yes* ☐ *No*

How has it impacted you?

When you read that your child is seven times more likely to deal with it themself, how do you feel?

What has made you decide you want to help stop the spread?

The fact that you bought *The Worry-Free Parent* says to me that you love your kids deeply. That you try hard. That you're thoughtful and probably really smart too. Also that you're at least a little bit of a worrier. And the fact that you bought this workbook says to me that you are committed to finding something different from what you're experiencing now.

How do you hope this workbook will change things?

Worry uses the past to define us. Worry distracts us in the present. And worry defeats us in the future . . . and we're not even there yet. Oh, and one of the most important things to establish is that worry lies. It uses the past, present, and future to lie to you about who you are and who you can be as a parent.

How has worry defined you in the past?

How is he (worry) distracting you from the present?

How is he already making you feel defeated in the future?

What are three ways you believe worry is lying to you today?

1. _____

2. _____

3. _____

I want you to hear me say again these words from the book: "You're doing a great job. Just the fact that you're reading this book helps me know that you're trying hard as a parent. You want to do all you can to love your kids. And you're brave enough to look at how your life impacts theirs. I truly believe from all my years of counseling that to look at your own life and deal with your own stuff is one of the very best gifts you can give your children."

> We all need to hear truth, but especially those of us who are worriers.

Worry-Fighting Truth

Because we know that this extraordinary day is just ahead, we pray for you all the time—pray that our God will make you fit for what he's called you to be, pray that he'll fill your good ideas and acts of faith with his own energy so that it all amounts to something. . . . Grace is behind and through all of this, our God giving himself freely, the Master, Jesus Christ, giving himself freely.

—2 Thessalonians 1:11–12 THE MESSAGE

Gratefuls, Hopefuls, and Truthfuls

Three things I'm grateful for

1. _____

2. _____

3. _____

Three things bringing me hope

1. _____

2. _____

3. _____

Three truths I want to remember

1. _____

2. _____

3. _____

To help you track your progress, I'd like you to answer a few more questions that end each chapter. Way to go on getting through the introduction. I wish I could hear what you're learning already. There's so much more to come as you understand more of who you are and all the good that you bring to the life of your kids.

TODAY'S CHECK-IN

1. What have you learned about yourself as a person?

2. What have you learned about yourself as a parent?

3. What has worry been telling you as you've read?

4. What has your gut been telling you?

5. What do you want to remember from this chapter?

6. What do you want to put into practice?

7. What are three ways you're proud of yourself right now?

Understanding the Past

1

Understanding Worry
and Anxiety

Let's start this chapter by answering these questions:

As you're reading this, do you feel worried?   ☐ Yes ☐ No

Do you have a stress level you'd rate higher than a six out of ten? What number would you give it?   ☐ Yes ☐ No #_____

Are your shoulders hunched up around your neck?   ☐ Yes ☐ No

Is your jaw clenched?   ☐ Yes ☐ No

Have you gotten frustrated with any of your children in the past twenty-four hours?   ☐ Yes ☐ No

Have you reacted with the same emotion and intensity as your child?
☐ Yes ☐ No

Have you had a hard time falling asleep?   ☐ Yes ☐ No

Have you had flashes of thoughts of your children being hurt?   ☐ Yes ☐ No

Have you had intrusive, irrational thoughts?   ☐ Yes ☐ No

Have any of those thoughts felt like they got stuck on a loop in your mind?
☐ Yes ☐ No

Have you had a worried reaction that was bigger than the situation warranted? ☐ Yes ☐ No

Have you had worst-case-scenario thoughts regarding your kids?
☐ Yes ☐ No

Have you felt like a failure as a parent? ☐ Yes ☐ No

Now, let's dig a little deeper. *How have you felt like a failure?*

What is a truth you know already to counteract worry's lie?

In chapter 1 of *The Worry-Free Parent*, you read about the podcast interviewer who said, "We're the first generation of healthy parents." *How do you feel about that statement?*

Would you describe your parents as healthy? Why or why not?

I shared that statement at a recent parenting seminar with grandparents in the room. One older couple got up and walked out immediately. For some of us, the parents who raised us not only weren't particularly healthy, but also weren't willing to look at their own stuff. Again, your parents were likely doing the best they could with what they knew at the time. Or maybe they weren't. *How would you like to parent similarly to how you were raised?*

What would you like to do differently?

You are forging a new path. And that path is paved with grace—grace from God and grace I would like you to learn to give yourself. If giving yourself grace is more important than trying harder, *what are three ways you could give yourself grace right now?*

What do you recognize in yourself from the following list?

- ☐ I'm aware of the things I wish didn't happen in my parenting, like how something inside of me is triggered when my kids are triggered.
- ☐ I can match their emotion and intensity, and do so more often than I'd like.
- ☐ I can get stuck in the what-if spiral.
- ☐ I get angrier than I wish I did.
- ☐ It can sometimes be hard to let go of my need for control and simply enjoy my kids.

23

Write about a time when one of the above happened and what you wish you had done differently.

Five Things True about Anxiety

1. *The more we understand about worry and anxiety, the easier they are to fight.*

What do you know about worry and anxiety as you're starting this chapter?

Where do you see yourself on the worry continuum?

We usually only have a reaction to our fears when presented with the feared object or situation itself. We're afraid *of*. *What are you afraid of?*

Worry is more pervasive than fear, but it's also more abstract. . . . We worry *about*. Worry comes in all shapes and sizes and is a normal mode of thinking for most parents. Not helpful, but normal. For some parents I see, I truly believe they consider worry a prerequisite to parenting. *How often do you find yourself worrying about your kids?*

What are you worried about?

Fear is adaptive. Anxiety, on the other hand, is maladaptive. It misinterprets threats, distorts our thinking, and often causes our sympathetic nervous system to react without sufficient evidence. Anxiety also causes our worried thoughts or images to get stuck. *When have you felt anxious lately?*

What was it about?

How did your body feel when you were anxious?

What did you do to work through it?

An anxiety disorder is different from anxiety in that it (1) is more intense, (2) lasts longer, and (3) interferes with daily life.[1] For anxiety to be categorized as a disorder, it typically needs to be present for at least six months.
Have you ever been diagnosed with an anxiety disorder?

Do you believe you've ever had an anxiety disorder?

What was it like for you?

What did you learn about yourself through it?

What did you learn that helped in your fight?

I want you to remember. I want you to remember the good that came through the hard. And what you did that made a difference. The same tools work no matter how anxiety manifests itself. More on that later. But for now, remember the good about you that emerged during that time. It's still true today. Your past experience with worry and anxiety will only serve to strengthen you in the battle now. And because this battle has to do with your kids, it might be the most important battle you fight.

According to the Anxiety and Depression Association of America, "Anxiety disorders develop from a complex set of risk factors, including genetics, brain chemistry, personality, and life events."[2] *What would you guess has contributed to your anxiety? How?*

2. Anxiety left untreated only gets worse.

The average age of onset for anxiety is seven.[3] Take your age and subtract seven. That is likely how long this anxiety storm inside of you has been brewing. And I believe becoming a parent strengthens the storm significantly. *How have you seen that happen in your life?*

Worry often serves a purpose. Many of us try to use worry as a coping skill. We overthink because we believe we're coming to a more helpful conclusion. Or maybe we believe worry motivates us. It energizes us to do the task in front of us. Maybe we worry to keep ourselves from being blindsided by bad news. Worry makes us, somehow, feel more in control. And, in some families, it can even be a way of showing that we care.[4]

How have you, maybe subconsciously, used worry to work for you or believed it could?

How has worry become a way of life for you?

How has worry interfered with who you want to be as a parent?

What about as a person?

3. Worry plays tricks.

At this point, I have no idea how many thousands of parents I have sat with in my counseling office. They're parents of kids of all ages and all circumstances who have come for help. I believe every single one of those parents has one thing in common: At their core, they're anxious that they're failing as parents. I believe it's an anxiety that undergirds every late pickup, every forgotten school note, every blown temper, and almost every normal day in between. And I would guess the same is true for you. The anxiety may not even be a conscious thought, but it's likely one that lies just under the surface and is tapped into all too easily. *How has worry tricked you into feeling like a failure lately?*

How did you talk to yourself when that happened?

Giving yourself grace is more important than trying harder.

4. Worry needs truth. And a whole lot of other tools too.

Anxiety distorts. It distorts our perception. It makes small problems seem medium, medium problems seem big, and big problems seem insurmountable. In fact, it's not even the problems that are, well, the problems. It's the stories we tell ourselves about the problems—in other words, the thoughts we have as a result of any given situation that might be considered problematic. *When have you seen anxiety make problems bigger than they actually are?*

How did the story you told yourself make the problem bigger?

It's the thoughts we have (the stories we tell ourselves) that impact our feelings, which then impact or dictate our behavior. Choose three situations you can use to map out the way the triangle works.

Thoughts	Feelings	Behavior

5. Every parent worries. Especially the good ones.

You worry because you care. You are conscientious. You want to be the best parent you can possibly be. But that care sometimes gets the best of you, and it's hard to turn the volume down. *Have you found that to be true? How so?*

Replacing those thoughts is going to be one of the tools we use the most throughout this book. Choose three negative thoughts you've had recently and practice replacing them with positive ones below.

Negative Thought:

Positive Thought:

Negative Thought:

Positive Thought:

Negative Thought:

Positive Thought:

If good parents get it right 50 percent of the time, according to psychologist Dr. Dan Allender, *what percentage would you say you've been hitting lately?*

How do you feel about reframing your failure in that way?

I think you're doing great, by the way. The percentage I would give you would be much higher than what you gave yourself. You're already fighting so hard. And learning so much.

The fact that you deal with worry and anxiety actually means you care deeply, you're trying hard, and you're getting a whole lot more right than you are wrong.

Worry-Fighting Truth

As you learn more and more how God works, you will learn how to do *your* work. We pray that you'll have the strength to stick it out over the long haul—not the grim strength of gritting your teeth but the glory-strength God gives. It is strength that endures the unendurable and spills over into joy, thanking the Father who makes us strong enough to take part in everything bright and beautiful that he has for us.

—Colossians 1:9–12 THE MESSAGE

Gratefuls, Hopefuls, and Truthfuls

Three things I'm grateful for

1.

2.

3.

Three things bringing me hope

1.

2.

3.

Three truths I want to remember

1.

2.

3.

TODAY'S CHECK-IN

1. What have you learned about yourself as a person?

2. What have you learned about yourself as a parent?

3. What has worry been telling you as you've read?

4. What has your gut been telling you?

5. What do you want to remember from this chapter?

6. What do you want to put into practice?

7. What are three ways you're proud of yourself right now?

2

Understanding Ourselves

Our past hurts mixed with present pressure often dictate our future fear. *What do you think about that statement?*

How have you seen it to be true?

This may be a hard chapter to work through. We're going to talk a lot about your past hurts. We're also going to look at the pressure you feel currently. But remember that those two things dictate future fear . . . not future reality. There is so much good and freedom and even transformation headed your way. Hang in there.

> If we don't understand ourselves and the root causes of our anxiety, we'll keep transmitting that anxiety to the kids we love.

Five Ways We've Gotten to an Anxious Place

1. Anxiety is rooted in our past.

Think back to your home growing up. *How would you describe the atmosphere?*

How did your mom handle emotions?

What about your dad?

What do you know about your family history, from a mental health perspective?

We know that anxiety is inheritable. *Can you think of a family member who may have passed it down to you? How did their anxiety come out?*

How do you see yourself similar to or different from them?

Now think back to a memory of your childhood—one that represents what things were like emotionally in your home. First write out that memory as a story. Then respond with what you think a counselor, or even just a wise friend, might say about the memory.

Your Memory

A Counselor's Perspective

My hope is that you hear a lot of kindness back. Whatever happened, that memory marked you. It changed you. And I truly believe Genesis 50:20: "You intended to harm me, but God intended it for good to accomplish what is now being done." God will use that very memory for good. He likely has already started.

Research says that many kids who grow up with anxiety have parents who

- are overly cautious of the world,
- are very critical and set excessively unreasonable expectations,
- are emotionally insecure or dependent themselves, or
- suppress expression of feelings and self-assertiveness.[1]

Do any of those statements sound like your family?

When we grow up with parents who are anxious, we often believe that (1) their perspective is normal and true and/or (2) we're to blame in some way.

Did you grow up believing their perspective was normal or that you were to blame?

How did that affect you?

How does it affect you today?

I want you to go back to that same voice—the counselor or wise friend. *What would they say in response to you now?*

I imagine they would say the same thing I would. No, it wasn't normal. It was a lot to live with as a child who couldn't understand. You needed the grown-ups to be your stability, rather than having to be stability for them. It was not your fault in any way.

More than two-thirds of children report experiencing trauma by age sixteen. And again, I'm not just talking about your kids. I'm talking about you. Your story is important. Your pain is important. And the way you coped with that pain has a profound impact on who you are and how you parent today.

How did you cope? By becoming hypervigilant? By trying not to feel? Trying not to need or want anything?

For most of us, our natural tendency was to try to escape what hurt us. We escaped by ignoring it. Avoiding it. By watching so closely that the same kind of pain would never take us by surprise again. Driving ourselves deeper into activities or distracting ourselves with not-so-great decisions. In other words, we learned to protect ourselves. We made promises to ourselves based on our experiences of hurt.

I'll never make the same mistake.

I'll never feel that way again.

I'll never trust again.

Take a few minutes to *write about a trauma you experienced growing up*. It can be a significant event such as a loss or some type of abuse. It could be something that felt significant to you, such as hurtful words from a parent or a bullying incident with a peer. It doesn't matter how "big" or "small" the experience was. What matters is how it impacted you. *What was it like for you? What has helped you heal? Or how did you choose to forget it? How did that experience change you?*

2. Anxiety maintains itself in the present.

Anxiety echoes from our past, but it also maintains itself in the present. In fact, Dr. Edmund Bourne says that maintaining factors are avoidance of phobic situations, reliance on safety behaviors, anxious self-talk, mistaken beliefs, withheld feelings, lack of assertiveness, lack of self-nurturing skills, muscle tension, stimulants and dietary factors, high-stress lifestyle, low self-esteem, and lack of meaning or sense of purpose.[2]

Which maintaining factors describe your life today?

One of the primary maintaining factors I see is *avoidance*. In fact, research says that the two most common strategies of parents faced with anxiety in their children are escape and avoidance.[3] It makes sense, but I have to tell you that it doesn't help. When we escape and avoid the problem it only makes the problem worse in the long run. You avoid the nighttime meltdowns by just letting them go ahead and sleep in your bed. But the more they sleep in your bed, the harder it is to get them to go back to theirs.

What have you found yourself avoiding that has maintained your anxiety or theirs?

We also use safety behaviors to keep our anxiety at bay. We check the locks or wash our hands or whatever helps us feel safe in the moment. But safety behaviors are also perpetual. The more we check, the more we feel like we have to check. What about you? *What is a safety behavior that you fall back on that maintains your anxiety?*

Anxious self-talk also perpetuates anxiety. *How do you talk to yourself? With anxious language? Negatively? Critically?*

How does it impact you over time?

We all have mistaken beliefs that underlie the way we talk to ourselves. They can be about our kids, about the world, or about ourselves. *What are some of yours?*

What did you feel when you read "withheld feelings" and "lack of assertiveness"?

Would you say those phrases describe you? Why? Is it just a lack of time to have feelings and opinions, or are you withholding them on purpose?

I do believe that the longer we withhold feelings and don't voice our opinions, the harder those feelings and opinions can be to access. Your feelings and opinions are important, even when there's not much time for them. They are important and worth expressing, which is one of the reasons I'm glad you're working through this book. *How are you doing with self-nurturing currently?*

What is the last thing you did to refuel spiritually?

Emotionally?

Relationally without your children?

What number would you give your stress level right now on a one-to-ten scale?

How's your self-esteem?

Do you feel a sense of purpose or meaning?

Out of all the maintaining factors, which are you more prone to?

3. Anxiety is always searching for context.

Think back over your life. *When you were a child, what were the things that you were most anxious about?*

What about as a teenager?

What about now, as a parent?

How does your understanding of context change the way you look back over your own history?

4. Anxiety is a response to cumulative stress over time.
Have your busyness and stress as a family become too much?

How do you see them impacting your kids?

How do you see them impacting you?

When you were a child, what helped you deal with your own stress that you'd like to have in your life now?

How could you create more space?

Let's do the bucket experiment here.

Write in the bucket all the things that are contributing to your stress. Write them as high as they are to overflowing, if that's accurate. (I'm guessing it is.) Then, *spend a few minutes praying and writing about what you could do to empty the bucket or relieve the pressure. Write out your prayer here.*

5. Anxiety breeds under pressure.
Where do you feel pressure as a parent?

How does social media contribute to that pressure?

What else adds to it?

What relieves it?

Based on what you've read about anxiety in this chapter, *what do you want to change in your own life or the life of your family?*

After reading this chapter in the book again to come up with questions here, it's made me want you to take care of yourself better. You are under too much pressure. Parenting is the hardest job you will ever undertake. You will fail and fail often, but you won't always be an ass. (I sincerely hope you're reading the book alongside this workbook and know that I'm quoting C. S. Lewis.)

> Parenting is the hardest job you will ever have. It will bring out your own failure more than any other job, but it will also bring you more joy. And likely more sorrow. Each are inextricably linked in our humanity.

There is a little person—or two—or a larger, smellier person (a teenager) who sees you as their hero. Yes, they still do, even if they never say it. And even if they roll their eyes at you. You're too valuable to them and to the world to not treat yourself with respect, kindness, and a whole lot of grace. God is using your past and even your failure to form you into the exact parent your child needs.

Worry-Fighting Truth

Every time you cross my mind, I break out in exclamations of thanks to God. Each exclamation is a trigger to prayer. I find myself praying for you with a glad heart. I am so pleased that you have continued on in this with us, believing and proclaiming God's Message, from the day you heard it right up to the present. There has never been the slightest doubt in my mind that the God who started this great work in you would keep at it and bring it to a flourishing finish on the very day Christ Jesus appears. It's not at all fanciful for me to think this way about you. My prayers and hopes have deep roots in reality.

—Philippians 1:3–7 THE MESSAGE

Gratefuls, Hopefuls, and Truthfuls

Three things I'm grateful for

1.

2.

3.

Three things bringing me hope

1.

2.

3.

Three truths I want to remember

1.

2.

3.

TODAY'S CHECK-IN

1. What have you learned about yourself as a person?

2. What have you learned about yourself as a parent?

3. What has worry been telling you as you've read?

4. What has your gut been telling you?

5. What do you want to remember from this chapter?

6. What do you want to put into practice?

7. What are three ways you're proud of yourself right now?

3

How Anxiety Impacts You

In my thirty-plus years of counseling, I've never seen parents feel as much pressure *or* as much like failures as they do today. I've never had as many parents in tears in my office. And I've certainly never seen as many parents who live in a perpetual state of worry. *How have you seen anxiety impact your parenting?*

After reading what you have already read, I want you to remind yourself why you worry about your kids. Not what you worry about for them, but what your worry says about you as a parent.

In case you're still struggling with negative self-talk and couldn't get to the "right" answer—and yes, there is one here—this is it: The reason you worry is because of your care, your conscientiousness, and your great love for these little and big kids in your life. Now let's look more at how that worry impacts you.

Five Ways Anxiety Impacts You

1. Anxiety distracts us.

☐ Have you ever found yourself not listening to your child because you're worried about what's happening next on your schedule?

☐ Have you found that you don't even remember the conversation you had with your child before the birthday party because you were concerned about how they would do once they got to the party?

☐ Have you found yourself unable to laugh and play with your kids, simply because of all that's pressing in on you today?

> When it comes to the kids we love, our worries take over and cause our short-sightedness to become long reaching.

How have you noticed worry keeping you from being present with your kids?

What could you do to change that?

2. Anxiety makes us attach future meaning to present problems.

I do see anxious parents doing a lot of predicting in my office. It's all well-meaning. It's all under the guise of prevention. But I believe it also causes us to get ahead of ourselves and to get ahead of what God is doing in the lives of the kids we love.

Where are you predicting the future in a worried way for your kids?

What did you previously see as a problem that you now know is just an area where they're still developing?

3. Anxiety makes us micromanage.

Merriam-Webster.com defines *micromanage* as "to manage especially with excessive control or attention to details."[1] According to Investopedia, "A micromanager is a boss or manager who gives excessive supervision to employees. [Uh-oh.] A micromanager, rather than telling an employee what task needs to be accomplished and by when—will watch the employee's actions closely and provide frequent criticism of the employee's work and processes."[2] Double uh-oh. Now, I'm not trying to call you out here. I'm just curious . . .

Before you started this workbook, would you have considered yourself a micromanager?

I believe parenting will be the most harrowing, hallowed, out-of-control eighteen years of life you will experience. And it seems to multiply with each kid. *Do you feel out of control these days in your parenting?*

I want you to think back on a time when you recently felt out of control. *Would you have said you were micromanaging then?*

What are the areas in your child's life that you lean toward trying to control more?

What about your own life?

What would you like to do differently?

Perseverating means that in the absence of evidence or even with evidence to the contrary, we simply can't let our concerns go. *What might you need to let go of in your child's life?*

What do you see first: what's right or what's wrong?

How can you focus more on what's right?

When we step in—micromanage—and fix the problem for them, we're telling them, with the best of intentions, that they're not capable of doing it themselves. In fact, they often believe we're telling them that they're not capable in general. And please hear me say this as respectfully as possible. I sit with so many kids whose anxious parents micromanage different areas of their lives. It does not strengthen your relationship. And it does not give them opportunities to learn. In my opinion, it hinders both.

4. Anxiety makes us angry.

I hope I haven't made you angry so far in this workbook. Actually, I'm okay with making you a little angry . . . or at least a little uncomfortable. When was the last time you got really angry with your kids? Don't forget that what's at the root of that anger is a whole lot of love for your children.

> Wounds from a friend can be trusted, but an enemy multiplies kisses.
>
> —Proverbs 27:6

I know we're not officially friends, but I'd like to think we are. The reason wounds from a friend can be trusted is because they have your best interest at heart. I can promise you I do too. I am holding your best interest, the best interest of your kids, and the best interest of your relationship all close to my heart throughout the pages of this workbook and the book that accompanies it. I want the best for you. And I believe the best comes when you can lay down the micromanaging and work through the anger.

When was the last time you got really angry with your kids?

How do you think it impacted them?

Anger is a secondary emotion, meaning there is something else at anger's root. It's often anxiety that comes out as frustration at our lack of control. *What do you think might have been underneath your anger?*

How did you handle it afterward?

How did you feel about yourself afterward?

I believe good parents have more shame around anger than anything else that happens behind the closed doors of homes all over the world. I also believe good parents get angry.

How does it feel to read that statement?

My hope is that it feels freeing. That it lets you breathe a little more deeply. That just knowing that anger is normal and that there is something underneath the anger will actually cause you to be angry less. More often than not, I believe you're angry because you're anxious. And you're anxious because you love your kids. You just don't want your anger to cause you to sin. Or your anxiety to make you less than who you are.

Anxiety feels like it defines us, but it is not who we really are. It's not who we have to be. And it's certainly not what God wants for us.

5. Anxiety takes away our warmth and joy.

Have you experienced this to be true?

Let's do the exercise mentioned in this section of the book. I'd like for you to make a list with two columns. On one side, make a list of who you are as your best parenting self. On the other, list who you are as your most anxious parenting self.

My Best Parenting Self	My Most Anxious Parenting Self

When do you feel more of each?

How does anxiety rob you of your warmth?

What are you sensing already that God wants you to do differently in your parenting?

Anxiety can distract you. It can make you attach future meaning to present problems. It can cause you to micromanage, and it can certainly make you angry. It can also take away your warmth and joy. But it doesn't have to. God is doing a new thing already in you. And I hope you're seeing just a glimpse of the good He is bringing about.

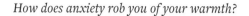

Worry-Fighting Truth

For here's what I'm going to do: I'm going to take you out of these countries, gather you from all over, and bring you back to your own land. I'll pour pure water over you and scrub you clean. I'll give you a new heart, put a new spirit in you. I'll remove the stone heart from your body and replace it with a heart that's God-willed, not self-willed. I'll put my Spirit in you and make it possible for you to do what I tell you and live by my commands. You'll once again live in the land I gave your ancestors. You'll be my people! I'll be your God!

—Ezekiel 36:24–28 THE MESSAGE

Gratefuls, Hopefuls, and Truthfuls

Three things I'm grateful for

1. _____

2. _____

3. _____

Three things bringing me hope

1. _____

2. _____

3. _____

Three truths I want to remember

1. _____

2. _____

3. _____

TODAY'S CHECK-IN

1. What have you learned about yourself as a person?

2. What have you learned about yourself as a parent?

3. What has worry been telling you as you've read?

4. What has your gut been telling you?

5. What do you want to remember from this chapter?

6. What do you want to put into practice?

7. What are three ways you're proud of yourself right now?

4

How Your Anxiety Impacts Your Kids

"God made you to do the hard thing in the good story He's writing for your life. Whether tomorrow is the best or worst or last day of our lives, we pray that God will give us everything we need to live it out to the fullest with courage and joy." This is the good/hard life. This is the way of Jesus. The way of glory through sacrifice, flourishing within limitations. And with unstoppable love coursing through the whole thing, it is golden. It will be hard, but we have already been made for the hard. God has equipped us with everything we need for the journey ahead, most of all with Himself.

Suffer Strong, Katherine and Jay Wolf

I wanted you to hear the words of my friends Katherine and Jay Wolf at the start of this chapter. God has equipped you for this good/hard journey ahead. This chapter may be painful to read and work through. But there is unstoppable love coursing through the whole thing. Love not just for your kids, but for you.

We've looked at how worry and anxiety impact you as a parent. This chapter is about how worry and anxiety impact your kids. And remember, I am a counselor who has spent thousands of hours with kids. I truly long for healing for you both.

Up to this point, how have you seen your anxiety impact the kids you love?

If anxiety is taught and caught, which do you believe takes place more in your family? How?

Five Ways the Anxiety of Parents Impacts the Anxiety of Kids

Let's dig a little deeper into the five primary ways I see moms and dads parent out of their own anxiety. I do believe all of us lean one way or the other. I'd like for you to really think and pray through where your anxiety shows up and how it comes across to the kids in your life.

1. Sidecar parenting

Sidecar parents believe that their experience will be the experience of their child. They are projecting their feelings and needs onto their kids, based on their own anxious past. As a result, their kids either jump on board their parents' perspective, shut down emotionally, or rise up to be the stability for their anxious parents. *When was a time you recently found yourself sidecar parenting?*

▣ The Premise: My experience will be his experience

Have you ever believed this sentence to be true? With which child in which situation?

▣ Where It's Coming From: My own anxious past

Have you found yourself thinking about your own anxiety while watching your child navigate theirs? When?

▣ What It Looks Like: Projection

Projection is when we displace our feelings onto the feelings of our child.[1] Have you found yourself projecting your anxiety onto your child? What were the circumstances around it?

Do you think your perspective could have been more about your past than their present? How so?

▣ How It Affects Them: They jump on board, shut down, or rise up to take care of us

How did your child respond when the situation happened?

What would you like to do differently next time?

2. Backhoe parenting

Backhoe parents are constantly cleaning up after their kids, believing that any failure on the part of their child reflects failure of their own. They are parenting out of their own self-critical voice and eventually lean toward being either a catastrophizer or criticizer of their kids. Backhoe parenting comes out as control and criticism, and children are left feeling criticized and like they can't live up to or please their anxious parents. *When was a time you recently found yourself backhoe parenting?*

▓ The Premise: Her failure is my failure

Do you ever find yourself wondering how their failure will reflect on you? When was the last time you felt like you had to clean up after your child?

▓ Where It's Coming From: My own self-critical voice

How would you describe the way you talk to yourself?

Do you lean more toward catastrophizing or criticizing?

How do you see it affect your child?

The way you talk to yourself will inevitably be the way you talk to your child. *How does it feel to read these words out loud?*

▪ What It Looks Like: Control and criticism
Have you found yourself controlling or criticizing out of your own anxiety?

▪ How It Affects Them: They feel criticized, like they can't measure up or please us
How has your child responded?

What would you like to do differently next time?

3. Snowplow parenting

Snowplow parents have children who would rather let you do the work for them than do it for themselves. And snowplow parents are happy to oblige. They do their best to prevent suffering for their child. Their underlying fear is that their child is not capable. Out of fear, they rescue the child, often communicating the very message they fear. It eventually makes kids feel incapable and hinders their growth. *When was a time you recently found yourself snowplow parenting?*

■ The Premise: I can't let my child suffer

All children long to be independent. And all parents long to help and even protect their kids from harm. *How do you see those two ideas coming together for you?*

■ Where It's Coming From: My fear that they're not ____ enough

How are you secretly filling in the blank in your child's life?

■ What It Looks Like: Rescuing

What is one way you've rescued your child recently? How did it go?

- **How It Affects Them: Eventually it makes them feel incapable and hinders their growth**

How did your child respond?

When we rescue kids based on our fear of their getting hurt, instead of recognizing their true capabilities, we hurt them more in the long run. They don't learn that they *can* do hard things, and they don't learn *to* do hard things. *What would you like to do differently next time?*

4. Helicopter parenting

Helicopter parenting is overparenting. Helicopter parents believe it is their duty to protect their child. They trust their child, but don't trust the world. As a result, they end up magnifying problems and creating more problems in their wake. Children of helicopter parents struggle with anxiety, entitlement, a lack of coping skills, and life skills in general.

- **The Premise: I have to protect you**

What does this phrase bring up inside of you?

▪ Where It's Coming From: A distrust of the world, more than my child

What are your fears about the impact of the world and the culture of peers on your child?

How might you be overprotecting them out of that fear?

▪ What It Looks Like: Magnifying

Have you been magnifying an area of concern? What is your motivation?

We set children up much better for life when we teach them how to cope, rather than how to see themselves as the victim who needs to escape.

▪ How It Affects Them: Too many ways

Children of helicopter parents have higher levels of anxiety, a sense of entitlement, and a lack of coping skills and life skills in general. They usually lean toward an unhealthy dependence or resent the involvement—or control—of the parent.

How have your kids responded?

What would you like to do differently?

Kids rise to the confidence we place in them.

5. Parade-float parenting

Parade-float parents are committed to the happiness of their children at all costs. They operate under the belief that if they can just keep their kids happy, they won't be sad or anxious. It's coming both from their own fear of reality and their desire to shield their children. Kids with parade-float parents end up feeling that their emotions are minimized. As a result, they dwell on those emotions or disconnect from and distrust them.

■ **The Premise: If I can just keep them happy enough, they won't be sad—or anxious**

Do you find yourself making decisions that prioritize the happiness of your kids over their character? Write about a recent time that happened.

■ **Where It's Coming From: My fear of reality and desire to shield my kids**

What in your own personal world is happening or might happen soon that you've been trying to shield your kids from? How is that working?

▦ What It Looks Like: Minimizing

Do you ever find yourself making the following statements?

"You're fine."

"It's not that big of a deal."

"You won't even remember this happened in a week."

"You'll get over it."

"You're making this bigger than it is."

"You'll feel better tomorrow."

Or even just try to change the subject . . .

> When we minimize a child's feelings, the child will either learn to distrust those feelings or get that much bigger with them to get our attention.

▦ How It Affects Them: They dwell on emotions or disconnect and distrust them

How do you see your kids responding?

What would you like to do differently?

Of all the above options—sidecar parenting, backhoe parenting, snowplow parenting, helicopter parenting, and parade-float parenting—where do you find yourself the most?

How could you start to change the way you interact with your kids?

How could you find more balance in your parenting?

What could help you be the calmest person in the room?

Worry-Fighting Truth

We who have fled to take hold of the hope set before us may be greatly encouraged. We have this hope as an anchor for the soul, firm and secure.

—Hebrews 6:18–19

Gratefuls, Hopefuls, and Truthfuls

Three things I'm grateful for

1. _____

2. _____

3. _____

Three things bringing me hope

1. _____

2. _____

3. _____

Three truths I want to remember

1. _____

2. _____

3. _____

TODAY'S CHECK-IN

1. What have you learned about yourself as a person?

2. What have you learned about yourself as a parent?

3. What has worry been telling you as you've read?

4. What has your gut been telling you?

5. What do you want to remember from this chapter?

6. What do you want to put into practice?

7. What are three ways you're proud of yourself right now?

Help for the Present

5

Help for Your Body

The first place anxiety shows up is your body. To do all of those wonderful things you mentioned wanting to do differently in the last chapter, we've got to start where your anxiety starts: the body. We want to understand what's happening and what we can do to intervene at the earliest opportunity. So we've got five things to *know* about how anxiety impacts your body and five things you can *do* when it does.

Five Things to Know about How Anxiety Impacts Your Body

1. Our bodies have a complex alarm system designed to keep us safe.

When our bodies take in a threat, the amygdala kicks off a series of events that sends our bodies into fight or flight. Where do you first notice your body registering fear? *Describe where it starts and the process you notice fear takes throughout your body.*

2. There are two primary pathways to anxiety: the amygdala and the cortex.

Amygdala-based anxiety starts in our bodies and predominantly impacts our bodies as a result. Our bodies, however, aren't the only place anxiety originates. We can also think ourselves into an anxious state—or maybe overthink ourselves into an anxious state is a better way to put it. Cortex-based anxiety originates in and impacts our thoughts, and it often gets our bodies on board too.

> The amygdala is immediate. It's illogical. But the good news is that it is also trainable.

If you find yourself stuck in worried thoughts, obsessing over doubts, reimagining ideas or images that only make your anxiety worse, or preoccupied with endlessly trying to find solutions to various problems, you are likely dealing with cortex-based anxiety.[1] If, however, anxiety comes upon you suddenly, without any logical reason or obvious precipitating event, you're more likely dealing with amygdala-based anxiety. To put it simply, cortex-based anxiety begins in our thoughts. Amygdala-based anxiety begins in our bodies. *Do you think your anxiety originates more in the cortex or amygdala? Why?*

When we have emotional and intense reactions that confuse us, it's often a result of amygdala-based memories. You may have heard the phrase "If it's hysterical, it's historical." That's the amygdala talking (or remembering and reacting). The amygdala attaches emotional meaning to situations, events, and even sensory data, such as sights and sounds. *Are you aware of any triggers you have for anxiety?*

3. The amygdala is notorious for false alarms.

There are two strikes against brains that have a tendency to worry. One is that they enlarge and develop a hair-trigger response in the amygdala. The other is that they create new neural pathways causing an even greater propensity to worry. Therefore, brains that are historically wired to worry will have even more worry in their future. *How do you feel about that statement? Do you believe it's true for your brain?*

Chronically worried parents react. Their first thought is the worst thought. And then that worst thought just gets bigger and bigger and bigger until it's hijacked not only their bodies, but their emotions as well.

Something's happened.
Something's wrong.
Something is wrong with her.
He's not like everyone else.
Why is she not learning more quickly?
Is he going to turn out to be a _____?

Where are you finding yourself chronically worrying these days?

4. The amygdala gets our whole body on board. And our whole family.

A grown-up's job is to be the calmest person in the room. And when our amygdala is setting off alarms right and left, the amygdala of our child will do the same. *When have you seen your amygdala react to your child's amygdala?*

What about the opposite?

5. Neuroplasticity works.

Neuroplasticity is the ability of the brain "to change its structures and reorganize its patterns of reacting."[2]

To change our amygdala's stress response, we have to be in the presence of what creates the stress response. We have to activate the neurons in our amygdala to generate new growth. If we're escaping and avoiding the things we're afraid of, our amygdala never has a chance to learn. *What have you noticed yourself either doing or not doing to escape anxiety?*

What is one thing you'd like to do differently?

> The primary reason that we don't work through our anxiety is that we don't practice the skills it takes to create new neural pathways.

Five Things to Do When Anxiety Impacts Your Body

1. Listen to your body.

As you know, the amygdala sounds the alarm within a fraction of a second. The sooner we can stop worry's progression, the less impact that worry will have on our bodies—and on those around us. *How do you typically first notice that your amygdala has been activated? Is it a feeling in your body? Or are you often unaware until your anger gives it away? Or your restlessness at night?*

Let's practice something together called a body scan. A body scan strengthens our mind-body awareness.[3] Start by taking three slow, deep breaths. *Where do you feel tension in your body?* Continue deep breathing by tensing muscles in that area as you inhale and releasing them as you exhale.

2. Breathe.

How did you feel different after that exercise? How could you incorporate more deep, mindful breathing into your daily life?

Breathing is like nutrition for our bodies.

3. Practice grounding exercises.

Anxiety lives in the past or the future. Grounding exercises anchor us to the present.

Out of the following grounding exercises, try to do one a day for the next week. Come back and write about how it worked for you.

Notice five things you see, four things you hear, three things you feel, two things you smell, and one thing you taste.

Name everything you see that's a certain color.

Run cold water over your hands.

Go outside barefoot and stand in the grass.

Name three things you see, name three things you hear, and move three body parts.

Take a short walk.

Squeeze a piece of ice.

Describe an everyday task out loud (as if you're teaching someone else how to do laundry, make coffee, etc.).

Count backward from one hundred by ones, fives, or sevens (depending on your math skills).

Try to remember your favorite movie scene by scene. (*Frozen* is a fan favorite in my office.)

Visualize a place you love and where you feel safe.

Pet or play with your dog (or maybe cat).

Picture the face of someone you trust and try to hear their voice encouraging you.

List your favorites of several different categories—food, TV shows, songs, et cetera.

Say three kind phrases to yourself that are true.

Memorize Scripture and repeat it out loud.

How did the grounding exercises impact your anxiety? Which exercises feel easier to fold into your daily life?

4. Practice mindfulness.

Mindfulness is simply an intentional practice of focusing on the present.

If we're lost in our thoughts almost 50 percent of our waking lives,[4] *where do you typically find yourself lost in thought? What are your top three things you think or worry about during that time?*

Let's practice my favorite mindfulness technique right now: the Three Doors Technique. **The Three Doors Technique** is one I recommend constantly for kids who are having trouble falling asleep, but I recommend it for use throughout the day too—for both kid and adults. In this exercise, I want you to think of three places you know well and where you feel particularly safe. It can be a vacation spot, your home, or even your grandparents' old house. I often use the summer camp I attended and loved as a child, Camp Waldemar. Imagine each location as a separate door. Walk through the first door and enter the scene. Use all your senses to visualize yourself walking throughout the entire place. What do you see? Hear? Smell? Feel? After you have walked through every room, exit and enter the next door. Then the third. Most people tell me they're asleep before they ever get to the third spot. *What are the three doors you chose?*

> The goal is not to stop feeling anxious. The goal is to learn that you can feel fear and still do the brave thing.

How did you feel as a result of this exercise?

5. Take care of yourself.

I believe one of the hardest things for parents to do is to take care of themselves. *What letter grade would you give yourself lately on self-care? What can you do differently to take better care of yourself?*

Let's do one last practice together. A few years ago I read about a breath prayer that has stayed with me. I wish I could find or remember the exact wording, but it called for breathing in kindness that leads to repentance and breathing out ways you're falling short of love. That feels like a great place for us to end this chapter. I want you to do the following for five full minutes. Set a timer. As you breathe in, think about God's kindness and love for you. As you breathe out, think of all the things about your day or week—or about yourself—that you want to let go of right now.

Your body is fearfully and wonderfully made. We both know that well. And so does worry. He will try to hijack your brain and body through that faulty amygdala. Don't let him do it. Listen to your body. Breathe. Practice grounding techniques and mindfulness. Take care of yourself. Sooner is stronger, and you are certainly stronger than any worry that can come your way.

Worry-Fighting Truth

Oh yes, you shaped me first inside, then out;
  you formed me in my mother's womb.
I thank you, High God—you're breathtaking!
  Body and soul, I am marvelously made!
  I worship in adoration—what a creation!
You know me inside and out,
  you know every bone in my body;
You know exactly how I was made, bit by bit,
  how I was sculpted from nothing into something.
—Psalm 139:13–15 The Message

Gratefuls, Hopefuls, and Truthfuls

Three things I'm grateful for

1.

2.

3.

Three things bringing me hope

1.

2.

3.

Three truths I want to remember

1.

2.

3.

TODAY'S CHECK-IN

1. What have you learned about yourself as a person?

2. What have you learned about yourself as a parent?

3. What has worry been telling you as you've read?

4. What has your gut been telling you?

5. What do you want to remember from this chapter?

6. What do you want to put into practice?

7. What are three ways you're proud of yourself right now?

6

Help for Your Mind

What are the lies you tell yourself as a parent?

Name ten anxious, recurring thoughts you've had in the past week.

1.	6.
2.	7.
3.	8.
4.	9.
5.	10.

Have you noticed when you typically have those thoughts?

What helps them go away?

If you're not sure the answer to that last question, this section is for you. We're going to continue to learn about but also practice ways to stop our anxious thoughts and fill our mind with things much better and happier and holier than the worries that can easily feel ever-present.

Five Things to Know about How Anxiety Impacts Your Mind

1. We all have intrusive thoughts.

Have you ever been aware of intrusive thoughts before? *What are the themes your intrusive thoughts typically take? Self-critical, worried, worst-case scenario, or other types of thoughts?*

2. The thoughts that get stuck get stuck for a reason.

Intrusive thoughts are predictable along the lines of context and your core beliefs.

Let's look more at the ABC model created by Albert Ellis:

A stands for the **activating event or adversity**.

B is for your **beliefs** around the event or **your interpretation of that event**. It's based on what are considered your core beliefs, or how you see the world.

C is for **consequences**, including both emotional and behavioral responses.[1]

Whatever we pay the most attention to is what's most reinforced. Your kids need you to pay more attention to their courage than their fear.

I want you to practice with three different scenarios, similar to those in the book.

Activating event

Belief

Consequence(s)

Activating event

Belief

Consequence(s)

Activating event

Belief

Consequence(s)

The more we can understand how our beliefs shape our thoughts, which shape our actions, the better we'll be able to change all three.

3. Our interpretations are what fuel our anxiety.

Cognitive fusion is when we confuse our thoughts with reality.

> Our emotions and responses are based more on our anxious thoughts, or our interpretations of the event, than reality.

I want to help you dig a little deeper into this idea. Think of a situation where your thoughts have become confused with reality. Let's identify each of the following components of the diagram:

$$\text{Thoughts + Context + Core Beliefs}$$
$$\rightarrow \text{Misinterpretations} \rightarrow \text{Anxiety}$$

It's particularly important that we identify the core beliefs, as those are where the change takes place. *When you think about your growing up, your Enneagram number, or even just thoughts you've had recently, what are three core beliefs you circle back to regularly?*

1. _____

2. _____

3. _____

4. *Cognitive distortions are interpretations based on our core beliefs.*

Cognitive distortions are negative thoughts that trigger both anxiety and pain. They're based on the very core beliefs we've been talking about. Dr. David Burns outlines several:[2]

1. All-or-nothing thinking. Those of us who lean toward all-or-nothing thinking often see the world in black and white, good and bad. *I'm a failure as a parent* would be an example of all-or-nothing thinking.
2. Overgeneralization. Once means all. Sometimes means always. A negative event becomes a recurrent pattern of failure or defeat. *My daughter had one panic attack* means *She'll battle debilitating anxiety her entire life.*
3. Mental filter. Many of us have a tendency to filter out the positive events, comments, or even thoughts and focus solely on the negative. *My son has never shown any responsibility. Why would I think he could drive a car at sixteen?*

4. Discounting the positive. It's not so much that we filter out the positive, we just give more weight to the negative. It has more power . . . especially if it's about us. *My daughter doesn't even like me. All she does is tell me what I'm not doing right.*

5. Jumping to conclusions. I believe we women are a little more prone to both types of jumping to conclusions: fortune-telling and mind reading. With fortune-telling, we believe we know how things will turn out, and (spoiler alert) it's typically negative, especially when it comes to us. With mind reading, we believe we know what others are thinking—and it's most often skewed against us as well. *There is no way she'll make competitive cheer . . . I'm a bad mom because I didn't sign her up for lessons in preschool.*

6. Magnification and minimization. We either blow things out of proportion or minimize them, including events or the way we felt in reaction to them. *She has the worst teacher in the school* or *He doesn't see anything I do for him.*

7. Emotional reasoning. Our feelings dictate our logic. I feel _____, so therefore I must be _____. *I feel like I've failed my kids* becomes *I am a failure as a parent.*

8. "Should" statements. Mental health experts talk often about our need to stop "shoulding" on ourselves. But we still do. We use words like *should*, *must*, *ought to*, or even *have to* in our efforts to make ourselves better . . . which ends up only making us feel worse. *I should spend more one-on-one time with my kids.* Or, *I ought to be able to manage three kids' schedules without dropping the ball.*

9. Labeling. This is another type of overgeneralization. Rather than saying, "I made a mistake," we say, "I'm a terrible person." Rather than, "I got angry with my son and yelled," we say, "My anger will ruin my son. I'm a horrible parent."

10. Self-blame and others blame. With kids, I believe both are present. *I'll never be able to do this*, whatever "this" anxiety provoking thing is. Or, *If my parents* [*or whoever*] *would just help* [*in whatever way your anxious child is often demanding*], *I wouldn't have to worry* [*or do the scary thing*]. I find that most anxious parents, however, blame themselves.

Other therapists have added to the list: outsourcing happiness, personalization (thinking something is your fault when you had nothing to do with the outcome), entitlement, a false sense of helplessness, and a false sense of responsibility to name a few.[3] *Out of the previous list, which ones do you feel like you lean toward more often? Write about a time you found yourself using one of the cognitive distortions:*

How did the situation work out?

What would you have liked to have done differently?

5. Rumination is the choice to stay in the distorted thoughts.

Our anxiety, or even our sadness, can become familiar and even comfortable, in a strange way. Any deviation from that sadness or anxiety can create more anxiety. *When have you found yourself ruminating?*

Are you aware of feeling stuck or making a choice to stay there?

How does ruminating sometimes work for you in the present?

Because ruminating makes us feel more in control, it often does feel like it works for us in the present. But ruminating eventually ends up working against us, as it leaves us feeling more anxious and often depressed. Plus, our thoughts end up becoming our reality. And those thoughts are not true.

> When we continue to think about a negative event, we lengthen our emotional reaction to that event.

Worry lies to us. It limits us. It keeps us from being present and keeps us from being ourselves. It also keeps us from enjoying the kids we love. But worry doesn't have to have the final word. There is good news.

Five Things to Do When Anxiety Impacts Your Mind

You are anxious because you're conscientious. You care. You try hard. Things matter to you. And, as we said before, it's hard to turn down the volume on all of that caring. We can't cure anxious thoughts, but thanks to neuroplasticity, we can change our relationship with them. Anxious thoughts may still be present, but they don't have to have power.

If awareness is the prerequisite to change, practice is what sets that change in motion. Cognitive restructuring has the ability to rewire the cortex, replacing those negative thoughts with positive, coping ones. Let's practice a little cognitive restructuring here.

1. Notice the negative.

Anxiety is found in our interpretations of events, rather than the events themselves. Our cognitive distortions become our reality. We want to notice the negative thoughts so we can replace them and can learn to be in control of the emotional reactions we have to those thoughts. *What negative thoughts have you noticed lately?*

Let's practice the downward arrow technique with an example of one thought.

$\downarrow$

$\downarrow$

$\downarrow$

Where does the thought spiral lead you?

Knowing that stopping those thoughts is where we need to start, what are some ideas you could use to stop your negative spiral next time?

2. Give it a name.

When we give our worried voice a name, we (1) reduce its power and (2) start to learn that it's not us, but a voice outside of ourselves.

I believe it's easier to fight that which is outside of us than within us.

What name would you like to give your worried voice? _____

He was a murderer from the beginning, not holding to the truth, for there is no truth in him. When he lies, he speaks his native language, for he is a liar and the father of lies.

—John 8:44

How have you seen Satan and your worried voice interconnected? How does that make you want to handle those worried thoughts when they come?

3. Disprove the thought.

We want to recognize the thought and name it, but we also want to disprove it. Let's use these questions with a worried thought you've had recently to practice being good thought detectives. *What is the evidence?*

Is the worried thought always true? _____

What is the worst that could happen?

What is the likelihood that the worst will happen?

Are you looking at the whole picture, or only part of it?[4]

We can also follow an if _____ then _____ thread. *Take another worried thought and finish the sentences.*

If _____, then _____.

If _____, then _____.

If _____, then _____.

Keep the ifs and thens going until you can't any longer. *Where did that leave you? Was the outcome really as bad as you had imagined?*

> We demolish arguments and every pretension that sets itself up against the knowledge of God, and we take captive every thought to make it obedient to Christ. —2 Corinthians 10:5

Try to practice either method of being a good detective several times this week. We want to learn to be good detectives and follow the facts, rather than our interpretation of those facts. And next, we want to learn to replace those worried thoughts.

4. *Replace the thought.*

"By deliberately thinking coping thoughts at every possible opportunity, you can rewire your cortex to produce coping thoughts on its own. . . . Watch for 'musts' and 'should.'"[5] Let's practice reframing thoughts by taking a worried thought and replacing it with something kinder and more positive.

*Negative Thought:*_____

*New Thought:*_____

We can replace or reframe our negative thoughts with positive ones. We can also replace them with truth. *What's a truth you'd like to memorize to replace your worried thoughts with?*

I want you to have truth in your toolbox that not only brings peace but reminds you of how brave and capable you actually are.

5. Stop being so hard on yourself.

You heard me say it in the book, but I believe it bears repeating: In my three decades of counseling, I have never sat with as many discouraged, weary, and defeated parents. And so many who are being profoundly critical of themselves and their parenting. *How do you feel reading that statement?*

I believe that when we're critical of ourselves with the kids we love, we get tighter and tighter and, in reality, angrier and angrier. The anger may be directed at ourselves, but it can't help but spill over onto the kids we love. Being hard on ourselves doesn't help. In fact, I believe it only makes things worse. *How have you been talking to yourself lately?*

What are some of the statements you find yourself saying over and over?

Kind, positive self-talk is one of the most fundamental skills we learn in therapy. And it is also one of the most life changing. *Let's practice replacing the negative thought you just wrote down with a kind, positive statement about yourself.*

If it's hard to get there with your own voice, we can always get there with God's. Notice the negative. Name the worried thought and disprove it. And then replace that thought with truth. Here's a good place to start: You are seen. You are known. And you are deeply loved by your Father—worried thoughts and all. His voice is stronger than worry's, and He is calling you to a much deeper and much freer kind of truth.

Worry-Fighting Truth

What marvelous love the Father has extended to us! Just look at it—we're called children of God! That's who we really are. . . . And that's only the beginning. Who knows how we'll end up! . . . So, my dear children, don't let anyone divert you from the truth.

—1 John 3:1–2, 7 THE MESSAGE

Gratefuls, Hopefuls, and Truthfuls

Three things I'm grateful for

1. _____

2. _____

3. _____

Three things bringing me hope

1. _____

2. _____

3. _____

Three truths I want to remember

1. _____

2. _____

3. _____

TODAY'S CHECK-IN

1. What have you learned about yourself as a person?

2. What have you learned about yourself as a parent?

3. What has worry been telling you as you've read?

4. What has your gut been telling you?

5. What do you want to remember from this chapter?

6. What do you want to put into practice?

7. What are three ways you're proud of yourself right now?

7

Help for Your Heart

Our hearts are soft, our ears open. Speak, Lord, of the change you desire to write into our life stories as they unfold. For we are gently becoming aware that knowledge will not be the basis for our understanding of how life goes. Love will. Amen.

Kate Bowler and Jessica Richie, *Good Enough*

As a therapist, I believe in the power of practical tools. It's why the past two long chapters of this book and workbook are filled with tools and ample opportunity to practice them. But I do not believe tools are the answer. Or maybe I should say, they're not the deepest answer. There are tools that can change the structure of our brains, which we all need. Especially in this day and time. But I believe what we need even more are tools that can change our hearts. That can bring hope. And that are not just reactive, but preventative in our fight against anxiety. That's where we're headed with the rest of this book.

On some days, being a parent requires too much with too few outlets. We lose hope and lose heart. Let's start with a look at your heart—at both where you are emotionally and what you need.

What do you need right now? Physically? Emotionally? Spiritually?

How is your anxiety these days?

When do you feel least anxious?

When do you feel most anxious?

When do you feel most like you?

When was the last time you were sad?

When was the last time you were angry?

When was the last time you were happy?

It's so easy to lose sight of the answers to these questions, or to not even ask them in the first place. When we don't stop to reflect on how we feel until those feelings come crashing in on us, they often take the form of anxiety. To be aware of and re-engage with our hearts is one of the best preventative tools we have in our fight against anxiety.

Five Things to Know about Anxiety and Your Heart

1. Anxiety demands control.

Anxiety loves control. Once we give in by avoiding the things we're anxious about, acting on safety behaviors, and doing our best to give it the control it demands, it only requires more. *What kind of relationship do you have with control?*

What are ways you feel out of control in your parenting or with your kids today?

What about in your own life?

2. Anxiety craves certainty.

Anxiety also tells us that we will only be okay if we're certain . . . certain of what's to come and certain of our and our children's place in it. *How would you finish this sentence?*

If I only knew _____, I'd feel okay.

Certainty isn't actually what we long for the most. Or at least the certainty we seem to be clinging to. I think what we want most is the certainty that God is in control. And, in that control, He is working all things together for our good and the good of the kids we love. Go back to the certainty you just wrote down, and dig deeper. *What is it you are really longing for?*

The next time a need for certainty arises, dig deeper. There likely will not be answers to the certainty we think we need, but there are always promises that speak to what we truly long for.

Go back to your answer to the last question. *How does God answer that longing with a promise from Scripture?*

Certainty can either make us more demanding (of more certainty) and anxious (when we don't get it) or lead us on the long, faltering path toward trust. *What would it look like for you to trust God more in this area?*

In the circle below, I want you to write down what you can control—what you're certain of. Outside of the circle, write down the things you can't control. They can be things in general or a situation that's currently making you anxious.

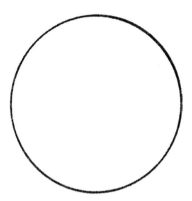

Now write out a prayer relinquishing those things that are out of your control.

3. Anxiety desires comfort.

As we talked about before, for your kids to work through their anxiety, they have to do the scary thing. For us to work through our anxiety, we have to do the scary thing.

What is one area where you've been prioritizing your child's comfort over their courage?

What about your own?

> For your kids to work through their anxiety, they have to do the scary thing. For us to work through our anxiety, we have to do the scary thing.

4. Anxiety requires predictability.

There is not a lot of predictability around us these days. Or inside of us. Any true steadiness or predictability in our lives is found in and through God. *What feels unpredictable right now, either around you or inside of you?*

How do the truths of Romans 7:15–21, Hebrews 13:8, and Romans 15:3–5 bring you comfort in the midst of that unpredictability?

> Jesus Christ is the same yesterday and today and forever. —Hebrews 13:8

5. Anxiety insists on avoidance.

Good parenting seems like helping your children when they're in distress. Anxious kids are in distress. And so, of course, to avoid whatever is making them anxious—whatever is making us anxious—sounds like the right path. But avoidance only strengthens anxiety. *What is one thing you've allowed your child to avoid recently?*

What have you avoided recently as a result of your child's anxiety?

What is one thing you'd like to learn to do that might make you a little anxious, but would ultimately make you feel proud and capable and brave?

Anxiety uses control, certainty, comfort, predictability, and avoidance to limit us. He lies and uses each idea to hold us hostage, requiring more and more of us and giving us nothing back but disappointment with ourselves.

That's exactly where we're headed next.

Five Things to Do to Help Your Anxious Heart

1. Go deeper than the anxiety.

Our emotions are always indicators that there is more to the story. *Go back to the last time you were anxious. Name three other things you were feeling at the time.*

1. _____

2. _____

3. _____

What could your anxiety have been trying to communicate?

2. Share your feelings.

> It's interesting that nowhere in Scripture does Jesus tell us any other emotion not to feel besides fear.

What is the primary reason you don't share your feelings?

Homework: Get coffee with a friend this week and share something you've been feeling recently.

3. Do the scary thing.

Let's practice exposure therapy together. We're going to use a training-wheels approach to something you've been wanting to do but have been too afraid to do until now.

Next to the top rung, write down the scariest-of-scary things you'd like to work toward. Then step down the ladder, filling in each rung, according to the level of anxiety produced by different activities that will help you work your way toward that scary thing. In the beginning, on the bottom rungs, the activities can be imaginal. With each step, you're going to practice your tools for the body, such as breathing and grounding. And your tools for your brain, such as reframing the thought. The goal is to stay on each rung until that activity is no longer anxiety producing . . . which may take weeks or even months.

4. Practice makes progress.

What is one thing you can be practicing this week to help you overcome your anxiety?

> When perfection is the goal, anxiety will always be our outcome.

5. Practice self-care.

I believe that practicing your own self-care as a parent has a much more profound impact in the life of your kids than trying hard to be a good parent. *How have you seen evidence of that statement in your own life?*

What are three things you could do to take better care of yourself physically?

1. _____

2. _____

3. _____

What are three things you could do to take better care of yourself emotionally?

1. _____

2. _____

3. _____

What are three things you could do to take better care of yourself spiritually?

1. _____

2. _____

3. _____

Proverbs 4:23 says, "Watch over your heart with all diligence, for from it flow the springs of life" (NASB). You are important. Your heart is important and worth guarding. May you continue to live with not only an awareness of that heart and what's happening inside of it, but a willingness to courageously carry your heart into the world. We need it. As do your kids.

Worry-Fighting Truth

Don't fret or worry. Instead of worrying, pray. Let petitions and praises shape your worries into prayers, letting God know your concerns. Before you know it, a sense of God's wholeness, everything coming together for good, will come and settle you down. It's wonderful what happens when Christ displaces worry at the center of your life.

—Philippians 4:6–7 The Message

And the peace of God, which transcends all understanding, will guard your hearts and your minds in Christ Jesus.

—Philippians 4:7

Gratefuls, Hopefuls, and Truthfuls

Three things I'm grateful for

1. ....

2. ....

3. ....

Three things bringing me hope

1. ....

2. ....

3. ....

Three truths I want to remember

1. ....

2. ....

3. ....

TODAY'S CHECK-IN

1. What have you learned about yourself as a person?

2. What have you learned about yourself as a parent?

3. What has worry been telling you as you've read?

4. What has your gut been telling you?

5. What do you want to remember from this chapter?

6. What do you want to put into practice?

7. What are three ways you're proud of yourself right now?

8

Help for Your Kids

What do you wish someone had told you regarding anxiety and emotions when you were growing up?

How would you finish this sentence: "My mom (or dad) always said . . ."

What are three ways you want your kids to someday finish this sentence: "My mom (or dad or ___) always said . . ."

1.

2.

3.

Five Things I Want You to Know for You

1. Whatever you are feeling right now makes sense.

How were your feelings handled by your parents when you were growing up?

What did that cause you to believe about your feelings?

What would you like to tell yourself now?

2. Your feelings are not meant to act as stumbling blocks but as milestones that reflect something important for you and about the heart of God.

What are your feelings today teaching you about the heart of God?

3. Feelings are not facts. They don't have to overwhelm or define you.

Describe a time you confused your feelings with fact.

What is a truth you could lean on when your feelings start to "drive the train" next time?

4. Self-care is not selfish.

Self-care means you stop waiting for others to give you permission.

What is one thing you can do today FOR FUN to take care of yourself?

5. You are loved.

What did you feel you had to do to be loved or to not disrupt the family system when you were a child?

How does that carry over into your life today?

If you were to fully trust that you are loved, what would look different?

You ARE loved. Because God is love. And there is so much grace, even in the midst of being your own personal pillar.

> May our sons in their youth be like plants full grown, our daughters like corner pillars cut for the structure of a palace. —Psalm 144:12 ESV

Five Things I Want You to Do for Them

You are the biggest agent of change in your child's fight against anxiety.[1] Here are five things I believe can change the course for you and the kids in your life:

> God is doing a new thing—but when we're anxious, we're often holding on too tight to see it. And that holding on directly impacts the lives of the kids we love.

1. Do your own worry work.

What do you feel like you need to do now? Is it time to press in on the practicing a little more? Or do you think it could be time to reach out to a counselor?

2. Let your kids grow and go.

What is one thing you learned through struggle or failure as you were growing up?

What was a way you got to experience independence, and what did you learn from it?

How have those things helped shape who you are today?

What can you do to let your kids grow and go a little more?

3. Have warmth.

How do you feel about the research on anxiety and parental warmth?

Would you describe yourself as a warm person? What blocks your warmth at times?

What are five practical things you can do to convey more warmth to your child?

1. _____

2. _____

3. _____

4. _____

5. _____

God can help you find your way to warmth, and He can help your kids, through that warmth, find their way back to you and to more courage and confidence in the process.

4. Offer empathy and questions.

> When we focus more on our performance and failures as parents, our attention shifts from our kids to ourselves.

If empathy enhances connection and questions imply capability, what can you do to infuse more empathy and questions into your parenting?

5. Let the bottom 20 percent go.

We build more currency with the kids we love when we use more yeses than nos.

Make a concerted effort to say yes more for the next week and report back on the difference it makes.

116

Let's look at your literal bottom 20 percent. *List ten issues you're struggling over most with your kids right now. List them in order of frequency of conflict or by degree of irritation they cause you.*

1.	6.
2.	7.
3.	8.
4.	9.
5.	10.

Practice this week letting go of the bottom two. Literally don't say a word about them. It's another way to have more yeses than nos for your kids. And for those nos to have even greater weight when they do come.

Do your own worry work. Let your kids grow and go. Have warmth. Offer empathy and questions. Let the bottom 20 percent go. *Which of those come most naturally, and which do you need to commit to practicing a little more?*

I truly believe those five ideas will directly lessen the anxiety in your kids and strengthen their sense of confidence and capability. I have a feeling they might do the same for you. And I am convinced they will be deeply beneficial to the relationship the two of you share. I can't wait for you to see and experience the difference.

Worry-Fighting Truth

May the Master pour on the love so it fills your lives and splashes over on everyone around you, just as it does from us to you. May you be infused with strength and purity, filled with confidence in the presence of God our Father.

—1 Thessalonians 3:12–13 THE MESSAGE

All praise to the God and Father of our Master, Jesus the Messiah! Father of all mercy! God of all healing counsel! He comes alongside us when we go through hard times, and before you know it, he brings us alongside someone else who is going through hard times so that we can be there for that person just as God was there for us. We have plenty of hard times that come from following the Messiah, but no more so than the good times of his healing comfort—we get a full measure of that, too.

—2 Corinthians 1:3–5 THE MESSAGE

Gratefuls, Hopefuls, and Truthfuls

Three things I'm grateful for

1. _____

2. _____

3. _____

Three things bringing me hope

1. _____

2. _____

3. _____

Three truths I want to remember

1. _____

2. _____

3. _____

TODAY'S CHECK-IN

1. What have you learned about yourself as a person?

2. What have you learned about yourself as a parent?

3. What has worry been telling you as you've read?

4. What has your gut been telling you?

5. What do you want to remember from this chapter?

6. What do you want to put into practice?

7. What are three ways you're proud of yourself right now?

Hope for
the Future

9

Admit Failure. Know Grace.

Do you consider yourself a perfectionist?

In what way(s) is perfectionism a strength for you?

Where is it a weakness?

How does it change things for you when people believe the best about you?

Let's go back to that idea of sitting together in my office. I want you to journal for a few minutes and talk about the things you would say to me. I want to hear about all the things you're carrying. All the pressure you're feeling. The lack of difference it feels like those things make. The lack of change you're seeing right now in your child. And, even more so, the anger you feel toward yourself for not doing and being better.

The title of this chapter is "Admit Failure. Know Grace." I believe so much of our freedom from perfectionism, as well as our kids' freedom from our perfectionistic tendencies, is found in these two words: *failure* and *grace*. *What are three ways you've failed in the past week?*

After each failure, write down the messages you said to yourself as a result of that failure:

I believe how you talk to yourself causes you more harm than the failure did in the first place.

124

Five Hopeful Things I Want Every Perfectionist Parent to Know

1. Good parents get it right 50 percent of the time.

What percentage do you aim to get right in parenting? What percentage would you say you're achieving?

I'd like for you to drop your goal—yes, I am serious. *What would the equivalent of a 94 percent grade be? A percentage that helps you believe you're trying and that acknowledges you are a fallible human being?*

Lowering your percentage can significantly lower the pressure you feel.

When we let go of the tight grip of perfectionism and allow ourselves the freedom to fail, we experience the joy of connection with the kids we love.

2. Insanity is repeating the same thing over and over again and expecting different results.

According to that definition, where do you see evidence of a little insanity in your parenting these days?

125

> Have some of you noticed that we are not yet perfect? . . . If I was "trying to be good," I would be rebuilding the same old barn that I tore down. —Galatians 2:17–18 The Message

How do you fall back into the trap of trying to be good as a parent?

What about as a person?

A reminder from your friendly Daystar therapists: Zoom out to the big picture of parenting. If your kid is aware that (1) you love them, and (2) they can trust you, then relax, because you're doing it right.

What are three ways you could zoom out currently?

1. _____

2. _____

3. _____

3. Practice more "oops" than "shoots."

A reminder from your friendly Daystar therapists: If you don't learn how to stop criticizing yourself, the criticism will spill over into the lives of your kids. It has to go somewhere.

Have you found the above statement to be true? When was a time you saw that happen?

Write an angry note to your inner critic telling him exactly what you think of him and how he impacts your life and your parenting. Use your angriest, bossiest voice. Using an angry voice with our inner critic can help us find a gentler voice to use with ourselves.

As I have more grace for myself, I have more grace for others.

4. *"We grow spiritually much more by doing it wrong than by doing it right."*[1]
Why would you guess we grow more spiritually by doing things wrong?

127

How have you found that to be true in your own life?

What could you say to yourself to help you move past the failure to receive grace?

5. Grace is our deepest need.

Our failures deepen our need for God. Your children's failures will too. Allow yourself to fail. Fail in front of them. Melissa Trevathan, in our Modern Parents, Vintage Values parenting seminar, talks about how "we can't be Jesus to our kids, but we can need Jesus in front of them." You are going to fail as a parent. When you do, rather than listening to the voice of the inner critic, listen to the voice of God.

What is a truth from Scripture that can bring you back to a place of grace the next time you hear the worry monster in the form of the inner critic?

Let's lean into that hope a little more with a few things that can help you, and therefore your kids, experience more freedom from perfectionism.

10 Hopeful Things I Want Every Perfectionist Parent to Practice

Again, no pressure. Just things to think on and failingly move toward. With God's grace. In hope. I'd like for you to take a minute to write a few sentences on how you can do more of each—with and for the kids you love.

1. Slow down

2. Trust the process

3. Savor the moment

4. Assume the best

5. Fail in front of them

6. Learn to laugh at yourself

> **Laughter eases the pressure of perfectionism.**

7. See their gifts

8. Encourage

9. Sit with the negative emotion

10. Remember that you are doing enough

It's not only that you're doing enough. You are enough. God knew you were the parent each of your kids needed—on your 94 percent days, your 50 percent days, and even your 15 percent days. There is so much grace. And we make that grace even more real for the kids we love when we can admit our own failure and receive grace ourselves. You are so very loved . . . by them and by Him.

Worry-Fighting Truth

Do not fear, Zion. . . . The Lord your God is with you, the Mighty Warrior who saves. He will take great delight in you; in his love he will no longer rebuke you, but will rejoice over you with singing.

—Zephaniah 3:16–17

Gratefuls, Hopefuls, and Truthfuls

Three things I'm grateful for

1. _____

2. _____

3. _____

Three things bringing me hope

1. _____

2. _____

3. _____

Three truths I want to remember

1. _____

2. _____

3. _____

TODAY'S CHECK-IN

1. What have you learned about yourself as a person?

2. What have you learned about yourself as a parent?

3. What has worry been telling you as you've read?

4. What has your gut been telling you?

5. What do you want to remember from this chapter?

6. What do you want to put into practice?

7. What are three ways you're proud of yourself right now?

10

Try Softer

Every parent with anxiety I've ever met is trying really hard. I believe that if anxious parents could try softer—not give up, but not be so hard on yourselves and drive and push hard constantly—you would be able to enjoy your kids and yourselves significantly more. The pressure you're living under is only hurting both of you. Would you say that's true about you?

Four Things I Want Us to Learn about Trying Softer

1. Here's what trying softer can look like.

How does trying hard impact you? How does it impact your kids?

When was a time that trying hard actually made things worse?

Are there certain things you say to yourself that let you know you've hit an unhealthy place in trying too hard? "Why do I always have to be the one who_____" kinds of statements?

Now let's do the exercise suggested in chapter 10 of the main book.

Write three things you're trying hard with (that you really can let go of).

1. _____

2. _____

3. _____

Now write what it would look like to try softer in each of those things.

1. _____

2. _____

3. _____

Next, write what you think the worry monster is going to tell you when you do.

Finally, write what you can say in response with your kindest, gentlest voice. The same love that is normally directed toward your kids is what I want you to direct toward yourself. It's okay if it doesn't feel natural. Just practice. In fact, I want you to practice this once a week over the next few months. We're growing new try-softer-and-be-kind-to-yourself circuitry in your brain. It will be challenging, but I promise you that it's worth the effort. You're worth the effort.

2. Let enough be enough.

Which of the following are true about you? When I'm anxious . . .

☐ **The concept of enough doesn't exist.**
☐ **I worry too much.**
☐ **I try too hard.**
☐ **I ask too many questions.**
☐ **I overthink.**
☐ **I overprepare.**
☐ **I "over-" just about everything there is.**
☐ **I do too many kind things for other people.**
☐ **I "never enough" myself into a place of exhaustion.**

What would it mean for you to let enough be enough in one area of your life currently?

> You have done so much. There is no one asking you to do or think or prepare more and more besides yourself. And my guess is that you'll still have the same outcome with a lot less effort.

What is a practical way to remind yourself to let enough be enough?

3. Embrace the ordinary.

Our culture doesn't understand the concept of enough. We've lost sight of the ordinary. And that is, I believe, one of the biggest problems we all face today. *What could you do, as a family, to embrace a little more of the ordinary?*

4. Rest.

When was the last time you experienced a real sense of rest?

What can you do this week to rest?

The intensity we're living in is too much. For our kids and for ourselves. It keeps us from experiencing freedom as people and as parents. It keeps us from joy. And it even keeps us from living with a sense of hope. Try softer. Allow enough to be enough. Embrace the ordinary. Rest. I fully believe if you could practice each of those ideas just one time this week, you'd know more Sabbath before you even got there. Let's try it together.

Worry-Fighting Truth

Are you tired? Worn out? Burned out on religion? Come to me. Get away with me and you'll recover your life. I'll show you how to take a real rest. Walk with me and work with me—watch how I do it. Learn the unforced rhythms of grace. I won't lay anything heavy or ill-fitting on you. Keep company with me and you'll learn to live freely and lightly.

—Matthew 11:28–30 THE MESSAGE

Gratefuls, Hopefuls, and Truthfuls

Three things I'm grateful for

1. _____

2. _____

3. _____

Three things bringing me hope

1. _____

2. _____

3. _____

Three truths I want to remember

1. _____

2. _____

3. _____

TODAY'S CHECK-IN

1. What have you learned about yourself as a person?

2. What have you learned about yourself as a parent?

3. What has worry been telling you as you've read?

4. What has your gut been telling you?

5. What do you want to remember from this chapter?

6. What do you want to put into practice?

7. What are three ways you're proud of yourself right now?

11

Trust Your Gut

To grow beyond self-rejection, we must have the courage to listen to the voice calling us God's beloved sons and daughters, and the determination always to live our lives according to this truth.

Henri J. M. Nouwen

Do you trust your own gut, as a parent? If not, what keeps you from trusting your gut at times?

When was the last time your gut proved to be right?

Can you name a time your gut proved to be wrong?

Regardless of whether you've trusted your gut in the past, we're going to practice now. I believe your gut, outside of your faith in God, is the most important tool you have as a parent. You need to learn to hear and trust it—for your own sake and for the sake of the kids you love.

Five Ways to Learn to Trust Your Gut

1. Quiet the voice of worry.

What have you learned that can help you quiet the voice of worry in your life?

2. Be in the moment.

We don't want our fearfulness of the future to keep us from being present in the present. *Does that happen regularly for you? What could you do to remind yourself to be more in the moment?*

3. Pray.

When have you sensed that your intuition and the Holy Spirit's voice are one and the same?

Write out a prayer asking God to lead you into the depths of who you are as you lead and love your kids.

4. Listen.

When we pray, we practice sharing our thoughts with God, and we offer them open-handed in dialogue.

Now that you've written out a prayer, I want you to have a little time to just listen for God's response. Or just to experience the stillness of God's peace. Set a timer for ten minutes. Listen. Don't judge yourself if your mind wanders. Give God room to meet you. And *write down what you heard or experienced during that time.*

How can you experience more time for both praying and listening for the Holy Spirit's voice in your life?

> Just like in our relationships, the more often we hear a voice, the quicker we are to recognize it.

5. Keep trusting.

Whose voice do you sometimes value more than your own internal voice? Why?

What could you do to remind yourself to listen to the other voices, but to realize that God speaks most directly to you about you—as a parent and a person?

God has given you a superpower of intuition. It is one of the greatest gifts you will receive in your life as a parent. And as a person. It is also one of the greatest gifts to your kids. Listen to it. Trust it. God will use that intuition to deepen your understanding of your kids, of yourself, and of His immense love for you both.

Worry-Fighting Truth

Therefore, since we have been justified through faith, we have peace with God through our Lord Jesus Christ, through whom we have gained access by faith into this grace in which we now stand. And we boast in the hope of the glory of God. Not only so, but we also glory in our sufferings, because we know that suffering produces perseverance; perseverance, character; and character, hope. And hope does not put us to shame, because God's love has been poured out into our hearts through the Holy Spirit, who has been given to us.

—Romans 5:1–5

Gratefuls, Hopefuls, and Truthfuls

Three things I'm grateful for

1. ....

2. ....

3. ....

Three things bringing me hope

1. _____

2. _____

3. _____

Three truths I want to remember

1. _____

2. _____

3. _____

TODAY'S CHECK-IN

1. What have you learned about yourself as a person?

2. What have you learned about yourself as a parent?

3. What has worry been telling you as you've read?

4. What has your gut been telling you?

5. What do you want to remember from this chapter?

6. What do you want to put into practice?

7. What are three ways you're proud of yourself right now?

12

Trust God

What makes it hard for you to trust God?

Courage isn't the antidote to anxiety; trust is. Have you found that to be true in your life?

What would it look like today to surrender to God, trusting His good for your life and the lives of your kids?

As we learn to trust, God moves us. He moves us away from our worries and, ultimately, toward Him. And that movement changes not only our lives, but the lives of our kids too.

Five Byproducts of Learning to Trust and One to Grow (and Go) On

1. From context to context

In Scripture, God replaces the context of our worries with the context of truth. He gives us the why behind not having to be afraid. *Find five verses in which we're told not to fear, and write out the context God gives as a promise.*

1.

2.

3.

4.

5.

Write out one of those verses that you'd like to memorize.

> God's kind words can become the truth we tell ourselves, rather than the worried thoughts that loop endlessly in our anxious minds.

2. From grabbiness to gratitude

What is an area you have been holding tightly to lately with your kids? Write down the "grabby" thought.

Reframe the grabby thought with a more grateful one.

We want gratitude to have more power than grabbiness. It will, with a little time, a little practice, and trust in a God who holds it all so we don't have to.

3. From fear to reminders of His faithfulness

Thomas Merton wrote, "For the grateful person knows that God is good not by hearsay, but by experience."[1] *What is your experience? How many of the things you've worried about in the past year have come true?*

How many good things have happened that you never worried about because you never would have imaged them?

What have you seen just by remembering?

What are five more reminders of God's faithfulness that you have seen or noticed recently?

4. From worry to wonder

Look back on your life—when was a time God moved you from worry to a sense of wonder?

How much did you have to do with that movement?

How do you feel now, looking back?

How could you live with more wonder in the present?

5. From pressure to promise

What kind of pressure do you feel right now?

What is a promise you believe God is saying to you regarding that pressure?

Let's do a final experiment. In these two columns, write down some of the transformation that has already taken place inside you. Where are you seeing evidence of God's movement in you as a person and as a parent?

From	To

6. *From trouble to trust*

> In this world you will have trouble. But take heart! I have overcome the world.
>
> —John 16:33

Anxiety weakens our hope. It lies to us, limits us, and tries to keep us from trusting God.

What are five reasons you're learning to trust in the midst of trouble?

1. _____

2. _____

3. _____

4. _____

5. _____

We started out the book talking about how anxiety does his best to discourage us about our past, distract us in the present, and defeat us in the future. But, of course, God answers not just context for context, but time frame for time frame.

On the *She Reads Truth* podcast, hosted by Amanda Bible Williams and Raechel Myers, the three of us read through Isaiah 43. As we did, we were reminded how in just a few verses, God speaks to our past, present, and future. He reminds us that worry does not need to have its way in any of the three. He has been faithful in our pasts, He is with us in our present, and He has gone ahead of us to the future.

But now, this is what the LORD says—
    he who created you, Jacob,
    he who formed you, Israel:
"Do not fear, for I have redeemed you;
    I have summoned you by name; you are mine.
When you pass through the waters,
    I will be with you;
and when you pass through the rivers,
    they will not sweep over you.
When you walk through the fire,
    you will not be burned;
    the flames will not set you ablaze.
For I am the LORD your God,
    the Holy One of Israel, your Savior.

—Isaiah 43:1–3

Past, present, and future. God is the same yesterday, today, and forever. He tells us over and over again, throughout Scripture, that we do not have to fear. And in this passage in Isaiah, He even gives you specific context as a parent.

Do not be afraid, for I am with you;
    I will bring your children from the east
    and gather you from the west.
I will say to the north, "Give them up!"
    and to the south, "Do not hold them back."
Bring my sons from afar
    and my daughters from the ends of the earth—
everyone who is called by my name,
    whom I created for my glory,
    whom I formed and made.

—Isaiah 43:5–7

God has not forgotten your kids. In fact, He promises that He will take care of them. I can imagine Him saying, "I will bring your children from the land of fear and gather you from the land of worry. I will say to pressure, "Give them up," and to trouble, "Do not hold them back."

He has called your children by name. He has created them for His glory. And He has done the same with you. In the past. In the present. And He's got even more in store for your future.

Final Worry-Fighting Verse:

Forget the former things;
    do not dwell on the past.
See, I am doing a new thing!
    Now it springs up; do you not perceive it?
I am making a way in the wilderness
    and streams in the wasteland.
                  —Isaiah 43:18–19

He is making a worry-free, transformed parent and person out of all of the good that He has already placed inside of you. And that is more than enough.

Gratefuls, Hopefuls, and Truthfuls

Three things I'm grateful for

1. _____

2. _____

3. _____

Three things bringing me hope

1. _____

2. _____

3. _____

Three truths I want to remember

1. _____

2. _____

3. _____

TODAY'S CHECK-IN

1. What have you learned about yourself as a person?

2. What have you learned about yourself as a parent?

3. What has worry been telling you as you've read?

4. What has your gut been telling you?

5. What do you want to remember from this chapter?

6. What do you want to put into practice?

7. What are three ways you're proud of yourself right now?

Notes

Why This Book?

1. Kahlil Gibran, *The Prophet* (Penguin Books, 2019), 34.

Introduction

1. Sissy Goff, *The Worry-Free Parent: Living in Confidence So Your Kids Can Too* (Minneapolis, MN: Bethany House Publishers, 2023), 11–12.

2. Reid Wilson and Lynn Lyons, *Anxious Kids, Anxious Parents: 7 Ways to Stop the Worry Cycle and Raise Courageous and Independent Children* (Deerfield Beach, FL: Health Communications, Inc., 2013), 35.

Chapter 1 Understanding Worry and Anxiety

1. Edmund J. Bourne, *The Anxiety & Phobia Workbook*, rev. and updated ed. (Oakland, CA: New Harbinger Publications, Inc., 2020), 8.

2. "Anxiety Disorders: Identification and Intervention," Molina Healthcare, citing the Anxiety and Depression Association of America, https://www.molinahealthcare.com/providers/nv/medicaid/resources/bh_toolkit/anxiety.aspx.

3. Judson Brewer, *Unwinding Anxiety: New Science Shows How to Break the Cycles of Worry and Fear to Heal Your Mind* (New York: Avery, 2021), 17.

4. Seth Gillihan, *Cognitive Behavioral Therapy Made Simple: 10 Strategies for Managing Anxiety, Depression, Anger, Panic and Worry* (Emeryville, CA: Althea Press, 2018), 132.

Chapter 2 Understanding Ourselves

1. Edmund J. Bourne, *The Anxiety & Phobia Workbook*, rev. and updated ed. (Oakland, CA: New Harbinger Publications, Inc., 2020), 41, 42.

2. Bourne, *The Anxiety & Phobia Workbook*, 39, 40.

3. David A. Clark and Aaron T. Beck, *The Anxiety and Worry Workbook: The Cognitive Behavioral Solution* (New York: The Guilford Press, 2012), 41, 51.

Chapter 3 How Anxiety Impacts You

1. "Micromanage," Merriam-Webster, https://www .merriam -webster .com /dictionary /micromanage.

2. Julia Kagan, "Micromanager," Investopedia, July 11, 2021, https://www.investopedia.com/terms /m/micro-manager.asp.

Chapter 4 How Your Anxiety Impacts Your Kids

1. "Projection," Psychology Today, https://www.psychologytoday.com/us/basics/projection.

Chapter 5 Help for Your Body

1. Catherine M. Pittman and Elizabeth M. Karle, *Rewire Your Anxious Brain: How to Use the Neuroscience of Fear to End Anxiety, Panic & Worry* (Oakland, CA: New Harbinger Publications, Inc., 2015), 14.

2. Pittman and Karle, *Rewire Your Anxious Brain*, 6.

3. Julie Corliss, "Six Relaxation Techniques to Reduce Stress," Harvard Health Publishing, February 2, 2022, https://www.health.harvard.edu/mind-and-mood/six-relaxation-techniques-to-reduce-stress.

4. Judson Brewer, *Unwinding Anxiety: New Science Shows How to Break the Cycles of Worry and Fear to Heal Your Mind* (New York: Avery, 2021), 86.

Chapter 6 Help for Your Mind

1. Kirsten Nunez, "What Is the ABC Model in Cognitive Behavioral Therapy?" *Healthline*, April 17, 2020, https://www.healthline.com/health/abc-model#how-it-works.

2. David D. Burns, *Feeling Great: The Revolutionary New Treatment for Depression and Anxiety* (Eau Claire, WI: PESI Publishing and Media, 2020), 65.

3. Seth J. Gillihan, *Cognitive Behavioral Therapy Made Simple: 10 Strategies for Managing Anxiety, Depression, Anger, Panic, and Worry* (Emeryville, CA: Althea Press, 2018), 56–57.

4. Edmund J. Bourne, *The Anxiety & Phobia Workbook*, rev. and updated ed. (Oakland, CA: New Harbinger Publications, Inc., 2020), 197.

5. Catherine M. Pittman and Elizabeth M. Karle, *Rewire Your Anxious Brain: How to Use the Neuroscience of Fear to End Anxiety, Panic & Worry* (Oakland, CA: New Harbinger Publications, Inc., 2015), 186.

Chapter 8 Help for Your Kids

1. Cathy Creswell, Monika Parkinson, Kerstin Thirlwall, and Lucy Willetts, *Parent-Led CBT for Child Anxiety: Helping Parents Help Their Kids* (New York: The Guilford Press, 2017), 3.

Chapter 9 Admit Failure. Know Grace.

1. Richard Rohr, *Falling Upward: A Spirituality for the Two Halves of Life* (San Francisco: Jossey-Bass, 2011), xxii.

Chapter 12 Trust God

1. Thomas Merton, *Thoughts in Solitude* (New York: Farrar, Straus & Giroux, 1956, 1999), 33.

Sissy Goff, LPC-MHSP, is the director of child and adolescent counseling at Daystar Counseling Ministries in Nashville, Tennessee, where she works alongside her counseling assistant/pet therapist, Lucy the Havanese. Since 1993, she has been helping girls and their parents find confidence in who they are and hope in who God is making them to be, both as individuals and families. Sissy cohosts the popular podcast *Raising Boys and Girls*, is a sought-after speaker for parenting events, and is the author of twelve books, including the bestselling *Raising Worry-Free Girls* and *Braver, Stronger, Smarter*, for elementary-aged girls, and *Brave*, for teenage girls.

More from SISSY GOFF

In a world fraught with worry and anxiety, veteran counselor Sissy Goff offers practical advice on how you can instill bravery and strength in your daughter, helping her understand why her brain is often working against her when she starts to worry and what she can do to fight back.

Raising Worry-Free Girls

This illustrated guide for girls ages 6 to 11 will help your daughter see how brave, strong, and smart God made her. Through easy-to-read stories and writing and drawing prompts, she will learn practical ways to fight back when worries come up and will feel empowered knowing she is deeply loved by a God who is bigger than her fears.

Braver, Stronger, Smarter

This teen-friendly guide—for girls ages 13 to 18—from counselor Sissy Goff will help your daughter understand anxiety's roots and why her brain is often working against her when she worries. In this book filled with stories and self-discovery exercises, she will find more of her voice and her confidence, discovering the brave girl God made her to be.

Brave

You May Also Like . . .

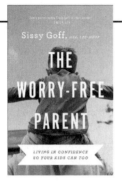

With over 30 years of experience helping both children and adults, veteran counselor and parenting expert Sissy Goff offers you practical, well-researched tools that will help you experience freedom from anxiety; raise confident, courageous kids; discover a more joyful connection to your children; and become a worry-free family in an anxious world.

The Worry-Free Parent